GUARD YOUR

HEART
& HOME

*Pursuing Peace
in Your Living Space*

GUARD YOUR

HEART & HOME

Pursuing Peace in Your Living Space

Victoria V Duerstock

END GAME
Press

www.endgamepress.com

Guard Your Heart & Home: Pursuing Peace in Your Living Space

End Game Press books may be purchased in bulk at special discounts for sales promotion, corporate gifts, ministry, fund-raising, or educational purposes. Special editions can also be created to specifications. For details, contact Special Sales Dept., End Game Press, P.O. Box 206, Nesbit, MS 38651 or info@endgamepress.com.

Visit our website at www.endgamepress.com.

Library of Congress Control Number: 2021937865

ISBN: 978-1-63797-002-7

eBook ISBN: 978-1-63797-003-4

Cover Design by Bruce Gore, Gore Studio Inc.

Cover Photo by Jenny Zacharewicz, IG: @bigfamilylittlefarmhouse, www.bigfamilylittlefarmhouse.com

Interior design by Erin Stark for TLC Book Design, TLCBookDesign.com.

Printed in India

RRD

10 9 8 7 6 5 4 3 2 1

*Dedicated to Rob,
my one and only!
Thank you for the
many years of life, love,
and laughter together.
You balance me
out so well.
May the Lord grant us
many more years
ahead together.*

Marriage Tip

Serve each other. Count your spouse as the one that God created for special for you. Life is both wonderful and difficult. Having a Godly, unselfish help mate makes life a fulfilling journey.

JENNIFER INGRAM

The Struggle for Peace

I have said these things to you, that in me you may have peace. In the world you will have tribulation. But take heart; I have overcome the world.

JOHN 16:33 ESV

Ultimately the answer to why cultivating peace in our homes is so difficult is found in the Garden of Eden. Because of the sin that entered the world, there is no longer perfection to be found on earth. In a perfect world, we wouldn't burn the bread, yell at the kids, or be angry at our husbands. But the world we live in is fallen, and we are too. In John, Jesus warned us to be aware of our own failure to be truthful and honest. This sinfulness will harm our relationship with each other.

Added to this sin problem is the fact that Father of all Lies, the devil, is also at work! I Peter 5:8 warns "Be sober-minded; be watchful. Your adversary the devil prowls around like a roaring lion, seeking someone to devour."

Marriages are under attack. Godly marriages even more so. A towering divorce rate is evidence that the attacks work, and the devil seeks to destroy each one of us and our families, especially if we desire to do God's will and complete his purpose for us on this earth. If the devil can wreck our peace, he can insert conflict.

Small doses of these things will regularly destroy, not fortify. Commit your marriage to the Lord and ask Him to protect and intervene!

Dear Lord, I thank you that you are all powerful. I pray that you will lead and direct us and help us to protect our marriage from the attacks that are to come.

Create a luxurious and romantic escape in your bedroom. Make a haven just for the two of you— a space to enjoy away from work and life's stresses. Soft bed linens, fluffy pillows, warm throws, and a sweet-smelling candle all make your room a comfortable place to land.

Prepare to Battle

Put on the whole armour of God, that ye may be able to stand against the wiles of the devil.
EPHESIANS 6:11 KJV

When we have advanced knowledge of a difficult situation, we can be prepared. Rather than being blindsided by the challenges of marriage, we can be armed with the knowledge that we must prepare now to deal with future trials.

One way we prepare for battle is by putting on the whole armor of God. Number one in your toolbox of preparation must be the conscientious, intentional choice to make God and his word your priority. You cannot have a kingdom marriage without it.

Of equal importance is prayer. Pray for each other, pray with each other and determine that you will not let any outside forces distract or divide you. Prayer is the ultimate weapon we wield in this battle for our marriage.

Additionally, we must work to memorize God's Word. I can't think of anything greater that can fix my mind appropriately. When faced with conflict, discouragement, disappointment, or challenge, if my mind is prepared with Scripture, I can see the truth of the battle clearly.

Be sure you are using all the tools at your disposal to fight for your marriage!

God, I thank you for the tools you have provided to face this battle for our marriage. Help me to be reminded to use them daily!

Marriage Tip

Plan movie nights, picnics, and cook or bake together. Be sure to make time for play. It's easy to stay so busy with work and responsibilities that we forget this important relationship element.

Power of Prayer

Do not be anxious about anything, but in everything by prayer and supplication with thanksgiving let your requests be made known to God.

PHILIPPIANS 4:6–7 ESV

We don't have to be married long to experience hard situations. Whether it's because of a move away from family and friends, or the loss of a job, or financial stress, calamity seems to be around the corner. Not long ago, we had a menagerie of difficult issues in the same week—termites in the basement, broken pipes, wheels falling off the tractor, and my mom in the hospital for a clot in her lungs. Sometimes the trials are overwhelming, and the aftermath worse because we wonder when the other shoe will drop.

In spite of all these things, we have the amazing power of prayer at the ready for us in our lives. Unfortunately, we often turn to prayer when we have exhausted all other readily available resources. A habit of daily prayer for the big and little things, pressing in with extended times of prayer and reaching out to God for answers, is a more effective use of our time than anxiety and worry. We need not fear we are bothering God with our small concerns and worries either. He is the God of all comfort and cares about everything we are concerned about. Now, doesn't that fill your mind with peace? Instead of trying to fix things or stew in the myriad of thoughts that worry and anxiety bring us, let's make it a practice to pray first. We can be assured that we do our best work on our knees.

Father teach us to rely on you for all of our needs today, and to turn to you first when we are overwhelmed and in need.

Mutual Love and Care

The husband should fulfill his marital duty to his wife, and likewise the wife to her husband. The wife does not have authority over her own body but yields it to her husband. In the same way, the husband does not have authority over his own body but yields it to his wife.

I Corinthians 7:3-4 NIV

Marriage is the place we are able to live out the truth of many Scriptures.

Specifically, inside our marriages we learn to treat others better than ourselves, show the fruit of the spirit of love, joy, and peace, and be patient and kind. Because of our comfort level in marriage with one another, this safe place to land can often be the place we reveal the worst of ourselves as we can easily neglect our spouse in life's daily grind.

If you are a newlywed, you may not have experienced any challenges to your marriage just yet because you are still in the honeymoon phase. That's how it should be, of course. Enjoy this season of newly married life and practice cultivating mutual love and care regularly. But when conflict comes—and it will—it's important to remember to treat our spouse with this sacrificial love.

A selfish type of love makes it easy to react negatively by withholding our love and affection for one another when our feelings are hurt, or we feel neglected, or our spouse isn't speaking our love language. Loving unconditionally means loving with our words and actions–no matter what. We can love through any condition–good and bad even sickness and health–when we live with this as our intention. We can love because God is love.

Dear Lord, help me to love my husband unconditionally, even when I may not want to. Remind me that dying to self in my marriage brings much joy!

Design Tip

For a cozy look fill your space with throws, decorative pillows, and an area rug. Nothing creates warmth like soft, textural elements.

JENNIFER INGRAM

True Love

Do nothing from selfish ambition or conceit,
but in humility count others more significant than yourselves.
Philippians 2:3 ESV

Can I be perfectly transparent for just a moment? One of the hardest things about bringing two independent, self-reliant, self-sufficient people together to become one flesh is quite literally the independent, self-reliant, self-sufficient natures that come with them. Trust me, I know firsthand!

Often, we just grow tired of always being the one to give, which is usually false thinking, but gets stuck in our brains anyway. I'm always doing the dishes. She never takes out the trash. I always have to take care of the baby. In reality we aren't the only one who does all those things.

True love is work. In a perfect world, the feelings of love could carry us through any difficult day or hard time, but the feelings don't last forever. The work does, even if those independent natures don't want to do the work or put in the effort sometimes. We have been led to believe that marriage shouldn't be this much work, when it really is work to build a new life together. It doesn't matter if you are bringing a past into a new relationship or if you are building from square one for the first time, true love requires a diligent attention to removing selfishness from the equation. Practice putting down the game controller, the laptop or the cellphone and give your spouse the attention he deserves when he is talking. Let him know he's more important than the other things you have going on. True love calls us to treat each other with humility and gentleness.

Father, lead us into gentleness and humility as we learn to love each other well.
Thank you for enabling us to do this work together.

Marriage Tip

Don't assume.
Don't assume
he understands.
Don't assume you're
communicating. If anything,
assume you're not.
Men and women
communicate so differently.
Our brains work differently.
That means we have to
work extra hard to
communicate our needs
and our feelings or they
won't understand.

JULIE LANCIA

Cultivating Peace Through Pitfalls

Catch the foxes for us, the little foxes that spoil the vineyards, for our vineyards are in blossom.
Song of Solomon 2:15 ESV

It doesn't take much to trip us up in the peace we long for in our homes. Whether we are faced with stress from an illness or job, bear hurt feelings, or feel pressures from parents and in-laws, many times we forget to be aware that these pitfalls can happen any time. Because these dangers lurk where we least expect, they can spoil the vineyard of our marriage.

A major pitfall to cultivating peace in our homes is expectations. While sweet romance novels or sappy holiday movies could be to blame, our view of what marriage is "supposed" to be can be warped. We should be cautious and seek to uncover what expectations we might have for our marriages. Two lives converging into a collective partnership is not simple, and too many times the slog of daily life can be overwhelming for even the best of friends. We've had termites in the basement, the septic tank overflowing, kids throwing up—all on the same day. You want to run far and fast on a day like that. No one writes this stuff in a romance novel—and yet it's real life that should be expected. In those times a hearty sense of humor will surely come in handy!

Pitfalls are rarely singular events! Many times, they arrive in tandem and can be overwhelming. Guard your heart and home by anticipating these pitfalls! In doing so, you practice cultivating peace for your heart and home!

Dear Lord, help us guard our hearts and homes with your power!
Draw us close to you and to each other!

Leave and Cleave

Therefore shall a man leave his father and his mother,
and shall cleave unto his wife: and they shall be one flesh.
Genesis 2:24 KJV

The countdown to the marriage ceremony is often filled with so many fun things. While the emotional roller coaster can be challenging to ride, usually we are okay with riding out those feelings because we are pursuing the end goal—marriage—together.

But what happens after the ceremony? What happens when the day is over, and now we make a life together? Often the conflict begins. Decisions have to be made about where to put the glasses in the cabinet, who cleans what, who makes dinner, and other daily tasks.

It doesn't take long to figure out that becoming one flesh is not simple. Often, especially in a close-knit family, it's easy to grab the phone and air out our grievances. A big vent session makes us feel better! But before we know it, as a couple we have forgiven each other and moved on, but Mama doesn't know that, and she's feeling all sorts of things about your mean husband.

Though the need to vent and sort through the feelings are very real and valid, leaving and cleaving means not running away when things get difficult. I personally find it helpful to journal and sit in a time of extended prayer. Prayer has always helped me work through my feelings, and through prayer, I have learned and practiced the art of giving those hurts back to God who can make changes for me–whether in me or in my husband.

Lord, remind me to come to you when I am hurt and frustrated
instead of going to family or friends. Help us resolve our conflicts quickly and kindly.

Marriage Tip
Laughter is the
best medicine!
Learn to laugh
and laugh often.
Don't take life
too seriously.

Enjoy Life!

Enjoy life with the wife whom you love, all the days of your vain life
that he has given you under the sun, because that is your portion in life
and in your toil at which you toil under the sun.

ECCLESIASTES 9:9 ESV

Have you ever noticed that enjoying the lives we lead is often easier said than done? Like the daily grind of dishes in the sink, fixing another meal, going to bed, and getting up to do it all over again sometimes drains the excitement of living from us? Having lived more than half my life in the sunny state of Florida, I tend to grouch through Mississippi winters.

Ugh!

Yet, Solomon encourages us in this passage to enjoy life. He specifically teaches men to enjoy life with the wife whom you love. So many people do that naturally—I think it's rooted in our personalities—some people just live for fun and excitement and find it everywhere. But for the rest of us, we have to plan to lighten up. Fortunately, I'm married to someone who balances me out. He keeps the humor in our home which is so beneficial.

If you aren't enjoying life, try to figure out why and then begin to build a habit of play and enjoyment. Enjoy time with each other—doing whatever brings the most joy.

Lord, thank you for giving us a partner that can balance us and
help us enjoy the life you've given us. Help us to remember to enjoy each other!

Lord, help us follow your plan for our marriages. Give our husbands the wisdom to lead and love well. Help us faithfully pray for them to have your mind.

Wives Submit

Wives, submit yourselves unto your own husbands, as unto the Lord.
EPHESIANS 5:22 KJV

Submission.

I know . . . I'm treading dangerous ground. But I don't want to avoid certain passages of the Bible even if they are controversial. It's God's Word, and I won't tiptoe. Rather I want to discuss and inform. While I don't have room to deep dive into all the implications, I do want to encourage you to read the whole context. In verse 21, Paul encourages everyone to submit to each other out of reverence for Christ. We all submit to Christ's authority in our lives, recognizing that He is all knowing and sees beginning to end!

Paul elaborates that wives are to submit to their husbands. This in no means limits our capabilities, ladies. It doesn't hold us down or hold us back, rather it still allows us to express our opinions on everything:

From the color of the walls, to the financial risk to which we expose ourselves.

From the city we live in, to the way we will parent our children.

From the way we put away the dishes, to the church we will attend.

Then, at the end of the day, when we have shared our thoughts, our concerns and our reasons, we leave things with our husbands as the one who will have to give an account before the Lord. This is a place of rest for us. Many times, we find we are in agreement, but in those times that we are not on the same page, we leave the decision with him, and then pray that the Lord will guide his heart and decisions to be in line with God's will for us. God's way is always the best way.

Marriage Tip

Be flirtatious! Don't stop those gestures, looks and fun you
had early in your relationship just because you are married now.

NAOMI MCINTOSH

Grace Upon Grace

Husbands, love your wives, just as Christ loved the church and gave himself up for her.
EPHESIANS 5:25 NIV

Perhaps you have not had to face disappointment in your spouse yet, but if you have, I want you to know that many times our disappointment comes from having created expectations they are completely unaware we have.

We wives expect that our husbands will come straight home from work and eat dinner, but instead they stopped to visit a friend, or went to the store, or tended to something else.

Or it might be the reverse if we work outside the home and our husband is home. We might expect that dinner will be on the table promptly at five, but we have no idea what their day at home has looked like while we were gone.

We expect our spouses to read our minds and anticipate our every need. I know it's hard to believe, but the reality is that our spouses are not mind readers!

I think this is why we need a reminder sometimes. Many times, a husband has extra responsibilities and can forget to be loving and tender to his wife. It's not that he doesn't think it or feel it, he just sometimes forgets to express it. Most women want to hear that they are loved. Even if your love language doesn't involve words, it is still comforting to know that you are still loved and treasured. Warts and all! Maybe you haven't heard those words in some time, let me encourage you to offer them first, to continue being loving and tender, and pray that God will do a work in his heart to say what you need to hear.

Lord, help us to love each other with our words and our deeds just like you love us.

Design Tip

A few "must-have" ideas when shopping for your living spaces: candlesticks, stacks of books, lanterns, picture frames, a vase filled with greenery or floral stems, a fiddle fig or olive tree, something old/found, bowl full of seasonal filler, chippy bookends or vessel, pottery, pillows, & a rattan basket for storage.

JENNIFER INGRAM

Speak Truth in Love

*Rather, speaking the truth in love, we are to grow up in every way into him
who is the head, into Christ, from whom the whole body, joined and held together
by every joint with which it is equipped, when each part is working properly,
makes the body grow so that it builds itself up in love.*

EPHESIANS 4:11–16 ESV

Speaking truth in our culture today runs the spectrum from wishy washy happy thoughts to strident voices screaming on the town square (or Facebook). Yet one most important thing is missing in many of these conversations. The quality of love.

Without love we speak harsh, cynical, or angry words.

Without love we don't say the hard or difficult things.

Instead, we run and hide, and the end result is not being fully known.

Speaking truth in love means being honest with one another about how we really feel and risking disagreement. Yet often, in those moments, we find more to agree on than not! I think this is because we have a tendency to imagine worst case scenarios!

Either result—saying angry words or not saying anything—is bad enough, but how much more so in our relationships? As husband and wife, we must be careful to craft our words to each other in such a way that we are continually speaking life. Yes, we must speak truth, but our love compels us to care for the way we speak, the words we choose, and the necessity of the point we are trying to make.

*Dear Father, help me to speak life in my words and with my
actions not only with others, but especially with my husband.*

Design Tip

Try furniture and wall décor in different places.
Be willing to be flexible and re-arrange things
until the room works for you.

Quick to Hear

Wherefore, my beloved brethren, let every man be swift to hear….
JAMES 1:19 KJV

Ever been challenged when listening to someone you love? Maybe they are natural born storytellers who want to share every detail of their entire day, when you are just ready for a nap or some peace and quiet at the end of a long day. It's easy to go through the motions of listening but by completing tuning them out, saying "uh-huh" over and over. Sure, you are sitting there hearing them, but that's not active listening.

Listening involves more than our ears. Listening involves our brains thinking through what is being said, from the nonsensical and mundane, to the important and heavy stuff. It's hearing what's not being said in an effort to understand the heart of the person speaking.

And perhaps most important to remember—active listening means sitting without trying to come up with your answer! Your solution, your argument, or next line of defense in a conversation should not be part of the equation. Really listening involves reflecting on everything you are hearing before you even consider what you want to say.

This is easier said than done, right? It's interesting that James encourages listening first in this series of things he wants us to do in this verse. Being quick to hear means that the next two should fall into line in order of importance if we are actively invested in listening to hear and understand and know our spouse's heart.

Lord, I pray that you continue to make me more like you and help me to listen more than I speak. Let me show love today by listening, really listening to my husband.

Marriage Tip

Make going to church together a priority. Church attendance and involvement is what anchors us to the Father and bonds us closely to our spouse.

JENNIFER INGRAM

Slow to Speak

Wherefore, my beloved brethren, let every man be swift to hear, slow to speak….
JAMES 1:19 KJV

I truly believe the order in which James lays out this verse is so beneficial to us as we try to evaluate our words. We are often quick to speak and slow to hear, especially when we are upset, or tired or hurt, and we fire back the first thing that pops in our minds. Yet following Christ in our hearts and homes dictates that we don't fall back on what is easy or simple. Instead, we must pursue peace by hearing what God's Word is saying to us.

Quick to hear, slow to speak. It's a juxtaposition of ideas, the exact opposite of what our selfish human natures want to do. It's counter to our sinfulness to be slow to speak. There's so much ego satisfaction in the one-line zingers and sarcasm, but what often begins as teasing can become mean and condescending.

Being slow to speak considers how my words or my tone might affect the situation I find myself in. If I'm already hurt or tired or frustrated, my words can add more fuel to the fire, dishing out the same hurt I feel. Instead, if I am cautious in those moments to be slow to speak, I will be more likely to speak the words I need to say.

Giving ourselves time allows us to see what has been said a little better and logic takes over from the feelings that stung. Being slow to speak is difficult, but we are called and challenged to live a life that is upside down to the world, especially in our marriages.

Dear Lord, fill me with the words you want me to say, not the ones my flesh longs to speak.
Let me be slow to use my tongue in a cutting and hurtful way to the one I love.

Design Tip

As you combine yours and his, inventory the pieces that you can still use so that your budget can be used to fill in the gaps.

Slow to Anger

Wherefore, my beloved brethren, let every man be swift to hear, slow to speak, slow to wrath.
JAMES 1:19 KJV

Having a short fuse in a marriage can be a devastating blow. Whether you or your partner have the short fuse because of the way you are wired or because of temporary stressors, small arguments, frustrations, or silly things can escalate out of control.

Anger often finds itself rooted in pride and selfishness. When I'm upset and angry with my husband, it's often because he's poked a nerve, one that I'm already stressed or frustrated with. I'm often hardest on myself, so if my frustration is bubbling like a volcano, the added pressure from my spouse can cause an eruption which hits everyone around me—my husband and children. Often, I don't see it until it's too late.

In our Christian walk anger has to be dealt with early and often. Sometimes it's justified, in the case of sin, but often it's not justified, and can become an overflow event that burns everyone like hot lava. A difference of opinion, a challenge of authority, or a simple argument can lead to a boiling aftermath of epic proportions. When the anger mounts inside, purposely step back and actively listen, determined to speak less.

Lord, I pray that today you'll demonstrate the power you have over the winds and the waves in helping me battle my sinful self. Take my temperament and change it to be pleasing and loving even today.

Taming the Tongue

So also the tongue is a small member, yet it boasts of great things.
How great a forest is set ablaze by such a small fire!

JAMES 3:5 ESV

*Y*ou don't have to be married long to know how true this verse is. It is easy today to recognize the truth of this verse. One scroll of social media on our phones testifies to this truth! Unfortunately, it can be the same inside the walls of our homes. We often treat strangers better than our loved ones. Those who live closest to us usually bear the brunt of our tongues. In this matter of our tongues, it is very difficult to control what we say. The consequence of a fallen and sinful human nature, our tongues seem almost hard wired to get us into trouble from day one!

Whether an argument, a secret revealed, or a lighthearted comment couched in a jab, the tongue can easily light a fire and before we know it, a full-on burn-the-house-down escalation occurs. Even without malicious intent a negative reaction with a sharp and quick retort dissolves peace in our heart and our home.

Being mindful of the power of our tongue is important in our marriage relationship. If we honestly work through disagreements before too much time passes, then we have the opportunity to work together harmoniously inside the four walls of our homes.

Father, help me to live harmoniously today with those you have placed in my home.
Help me temper my reactions with the power of the Holy Spirit.

Marriage Tip
Do things to make your
spouse's life easier.

NAOMI MCINTOSH

Power of the Tongue

The tongue has the power of life and death, and those who love it will eat its fruit.
PROVERBS 18:21 NIV

It's easy to forget that our tongues have power. Power to build up or power to destroy. Often in our first few weeks or months of marriage, we maintain verbal control, but over time as we become more comfortable with each other and our relationship, we enter the danger zone. This danger zone is the comfort we find within our relationship and this security provides and supplies the opportunity to speak words that can destroy easily. Often, we find ourselves saying things to each other that we would never say to someone else.

Understanding that the real power to build up and encourage our spouse lies within us, we should be intentional with our words. We can find ways to build up our husband with encouragement, with respect, and with love. Speaking to him gently and lovingly is part of our job as a helpmeet! Although I understand if you don't feel particularly loving, especially in the midst of a difficult season, when we are sure that our words are gracious, we can defer a lot of negative reactions. Use your power wisely. Build up and edify rather than tear down and destroy. It's absolutely essential!

Dear Lord, remind me that life and death are in the power of the tongue
and to use that power wisely! Thank you for your faithfulness
and promise to provide just what I need.

Always forgive. Holding
on to anger or resentment
is the most certain way to
weaken a marriage.
Resentment is like
a disease that eats away
at the very foundation.
Communicate your feelings.
Nip resentment in the bud.
Don't let it take hold.
And as Jesus forgives,
let go and forgive.
It's essential to your
own happiness as well
as your marriage.

JULIE LANCIA

Blessing and Cursing

Out of the same mouth come praise and cursing. My brothers and sisters, this should not be.
JAMES 3:10 NIV

A fountain of water never produces both disgusting poisonous water and clear spring water at the same time. In much the same way, our mouths can betray a poisonous center of our hearts indicating a lack of spiritual discipline. The Bible talks often about being rooted and grounded in love, and about the fruit of the spirit displayed in our lives. We are known by our fruit and how it demonstrates growth in our relationships with God and our husbands.

Understanding the need for spiritual discipline as it relates specifically to our tongues helps us deal with the truth about our selfish sinful hearts. I'm sure you've heard the old adage "garbage in, garbage out." It really is so true—what's in our heart overflows, and if we haven't been careful to cultivate what's true and holy and just, we will often display what's false, sinful, and unkind. We can't expect to overflow love if our hearts are full of hate. We can't expect to extend grace to our spouse if we haven't seen the beauty of grace manifested in our own lives. We can't expect to overflow with kindness or mercy if we sit and steep in the ugliness of our negative thoughts.

We cannot overflow with both blessing and cursing. If you find yourself overwhelmed with negativity and feeling bogged down, check your source. Are you filling yourself with the milk and meat of God's Word, or are you being satisfied by the garbage the world has to offer? If you don't like your output, switch your supply!

Lord, control the overflow of my mouth today. Let me be a blessing to others.

Design Tip

If you find that you are "creatively stuck" with a room or space then take a picture. I have found nothing more helpful than examining spaces through the lens of a camera to give me the truth and inspiration.

JENNIFER INGRAM

Plant Peace

But the wisdom from above is first pure, then peaceable, gentle, open to reason,
full of mercy and good fruits, impartial and sincere.
And a harvest of righteousness is sown in peace by those who make peace.

JAMES 3:17–18 ESV

The idea of harvest, sowing and reaping, is found throughout the Bible and once again such a great visual example for those of us who learn this way! Whether we have planted a small home garden or farmed large fields, this commonsense approach makes sense in the context of our hearts and homes as well.

Sowing peace might mean setting aside our own desires. It might mean putting an end to my laziness or releasing a my-way-or-the-highway mentality. It might mean being kind when we've been treated unkindly. It might mean setting aside my own ambition for a time, to do what is necessary for my marriage to succeed. These things do not make us a doormat, rather this conscious practice of laying down dreams or expectations for a season provides a selfless act which cultivates peace in our homes.

I love how James applies the word picture "a harvest of righteousness sown in peace by those who make peace," indicating that peace is part of an action, an intention. It's also a fruit of the spirit and something the Holy Spirit grows within us, and at the same time, it is something we can cultivate. When we sow peace because we are peacemakers, we can see this harvest of righteousness in our marriages. What could God do with a peaceful marriage in our society today? A peaceful marriage provides light in the midst of the darkness to the world around us.

Lord, I pray you'll help me today plant seeds of peace
that will grow into a fruitful harvest in our home.

Learn the art of compromise. Make sure that you get to share equally in the setup of your home. Being careful not to clash, of course, but finding as many ways to agree along the way as possible will definitely bring peace to your space!

Jealousy and Selfish Ambition

But if you have bitter jealousy and selfish ambition in your hearts, do not boast and be false to the truth. This is not the wisdom that comes down from above, but is earthly, unspiritual, demonic. For where jealousy and selfish ambition exist, there will be disorder and every vile practice.

JAMES 3:14–16 ESV

James describes disorder in this passage as the outcome of a place where jealousy and selfish ambition reside. Are you struggling in your marriage? Do you have fights that never seem to end or mounting frustrations that make you want to call it quits?

Don't be surprised. You are not alone, and you are not the only one who is going through it. Whether you've been married a short time or for a few years or decades, please remember that marriage takes work. This work requires dying to self and many times we just don't want to. It requires setting aside my rights or what I believe I'm owed and being willing to take a step back to do what's best in our relationship.

Do you find yourself jealous of your spouse? Perhaps it's a job or position of recognition that he achieves. Perhaps it's a winning personality or an ease of making conversation that is harder for you. Whatever the case, recognize this as sinful behavior and confess it. Likewise, it's not wrong to want to improve yourself and your position, but there's a fine line when you become selfish in your ambition and decide it's worth it any cost—especially when it's damaging to our marriage.

Putting these things—jealousy and selfish ambition—aside can be a way to draw you closer in your relationship to each other and build a foundation rooted in the truth of God's Word.

Give me a heart, Lord, to follow you obediently no matter what.
Help me trust your plan is for my good and your glory.

Design Tip

Don't be super-trendy. Purchase things that speak to you, not what speaks to others. There are ways to incorporate a "trendy" piece into your timeless, classic style (i.e., wood signs) that won't make it feel like you live in a Cracker Barrel store. Subtle is the way to go!

JENNIFER INGRAM

Not So Cute

For as the body is one, and hath many members, and all the members of that one body,
being many, are one body: so also is Christ...

I Corinthians 12:12 KJV

The very character traits that drew us to each other on those first dates, into the dating relationship, through blissful engagement, and finally down the marriage aisle, can be what drives us crazy after many years into a marriage relationship.

Over time, these things we thought were cute or funny become bigger issues than we realized. Or the fact that we often go into marriages thinking we are going to change someone to think or be more like us. I can assure you that this kind of thinking will land us into a whole lot of conflict.

Just as I Corinthians 12:12 reminds us that in a functioning church body, not everyone thinks the same or acts the same. Not everyone has the same gifts or talents. These are actually good things! The same also applies in our marriages. We do not have to be just like one another to get along or make decisions. Instead, we learn to rely on each other's strengths to do what we can't, while they learn to work with us in our strengths as well.

We must always believe that our partner is gifted in the way God designed him and, because of that gifting, we can fully support him. He was made in God's image, and while he isn't perfect here on this earth, he has value and merit and should be given space to be all the God has intended for him to be.

Lord, help me to be everything you intend me to be.
Make me faithful to pray that my spouse is everything you intend him to be as well.

Design Tip

Choose neutrals and light colors for your main color scheme.
Then decorate with pops of color that you both love. The light colors
keep small spaces open and airy and give you a neutral palette to work
with to make changes as you grow and change.

Trustworthy

Who can find a virtuous woman? for her price is far above rubies. The heart of her husband doth safely trust in her, so that he shall have no need of spoil.

PROVERBS 31:10–11 KJV

Trust in marriage is an absolute necessity. There are too many trials and temptations in life to navigate without a safe place of trust. Believing that we are in the battle together, we trust that the other has our back. This is such an important part of balancing this life together.

I find it interesting in today's passage that the words clearly identify that the husband trusts his wife. In reading the rest of chapter 31, rather than a checklist of items to measure up to, you'll find a compilation of ways that we as wives provide value and substance in our marriages. Yet trust is toward the top of that list. And what is more valuable than trust? He can trust that we have his best interests at heart. Trust that we will love him no matter what. Trust that we will not harm him intentionally. Trust that we will seek to benefit him.

Having trust in our marriage relationship is absolutely essential, and if it's been damaged already, we have the opportunity to repair it with a new trust. Build trust by being open and accountable with each other about everything from spending to social media and everything in between!

God, I pray that you will help me be trustworthy in all of my actions.
Help us to build trust together ensuring a strong foundation for our future.

Design Tip

When deciding on a color palette find inspiration from something you love—a piece of art, jewelry or clothing.

Rainy Days

A quarrelsome wife is like the dripping of a leaky roof in a rainstorm;
restraining her is like restraining the wind or grasping oil with the hand.

PROVERBS 27:15 NIV

The proverbial nagging wife. Ugh! I know I work really hard to avoid being that woman. You too? Sometimes it feels difficult to know where the line is between making a request, giving a reminder, or being a nag! Or how do we avoid being quarrelsome when we don't feel listened to, heard, or acknowledged?

It's true. I wish I had some magical insight here or some deep-rooted wisdom to help us avoid this scenario, yet the Bible is clear about not being that nagging wife. Don't be her. Avoid it! Which means if we find ourselves nagging and arguing frequently, we have to stop. End of sentence. End of discussion.

While easier said than done though, I believe this is one thing that we have to practice faithfully doing. Make a request and offer a reminder, then leave the rest in God's hands. If we are faithfully praying for our husbands, we rest knowing the results are in God's hands. He will supply and will do more than we can. We certainly don't want to drive a wedge into our relationship by continually arguing or nagging. Take your reminders to the Lord and leave them there.

I pray, dear Lord, that you will help me to recognize
when I cross the line between helpful reminders and nagging.

Sexual Purity

Let marriage be held in honor among all, and let the marriage bed be undefiled,
for God will judge the sexually immoral and adulterous.

HEBREWS 13:4 ESV

Sometimes those of us who have grown up in church forget that not everyone else has, nor is everyone in the same place in their spiritual journey. In our churches today we find that marriage has started to look more like the world because we haven't been faithful to put the principles God's Word teaches us into practice regarding sex, adultery and even divorce.

Faithfulness in marriage is an important part of our covenant relationship. Building trust into our relationship comes from not breaking the covenant with each other. The pull to relax the conditions that the Bible puts on our marriages is ever so strong because of what the world has normalized in our culture, but please let me encourage you today to be grounded in what the Bible teaches. Marriage is to be held in honor and the marriage bed undefiled, sacred ground between man and wife.

Sex outside the boundaries of our marriage—pre-marital sex or extra-marital sex—is wrong and goes against our Creator's perfect plan for us. By preserving and honoring the boundaries of our marriages, God honors and blesses our union. There is less stress, less difficulty, less trauma, less hurt, and less pain when we establish clear boundaries and practice purity because of what the Bible teaches.

Lord, keep us pure and holy in our physical intimacy with each other
understanding that God's Word provides the perfect blueprint for our marriages.

Go on date nights. Just because you are now married, doesn't mean you should stop doing the things you enjoyed before— like dating!

NAOMI MCINTOSH

Love and Respect

However, let each one of you love his wife as himself,
and let the wife see that she respects her husband.

EPHESIANS 5:33 ESV

In the circle of a healthy marriage, we need to remember that husbands are to love their wives as Christ loved the church and wives are to respect their husbands. Love and respect flow freely when the marriage relationship is functioning optimally; however, when something gets in the way of that, those expressions of love and respect quickly shut down.

It is hard to express love to someone we are frustrated with, and it's equally difficult to offer respect to someone when we are angry. Depending on your personality, walking in love or respect might be a challenge. As a man you might have a difficult time expressing outward signs of affection to your wife. If you are a woman who likes to take charge, you might find a great challenge in this arena especially in areas in which you believe your husband is wrong. The difficulty for us both is to relinquish our rights and bring our feelings and expectations to the Lord. When we ask for him to help us show love and respect to each other even if our feelings don't quite match up yet, He promises to supply that need.

Depending and resting on Christ's power is important I believe because it manifests the truth of doing all things through Christ which strengthens me.

Lord, let me fulfill the vows I made for our marriage to love and honor my husband.
Help me to show respect and love no matter what is going on or how I feel on any given day.

In our home let love abide and bless those who step inside

A Good Thing

Whoso findeth a wife findeth a good thing, and obtaineth favour of the LORD.
PROVERBS 18:22 KJV

When Adam was alone in the garden, God saw he needed a partner and formed Eve from Adam's side to be a helpmeet. Proverbs reminds us that a wife is a good thing. Marriage exists because of God's favor and blessing and as part of God's plan for mankind, we are each given our part to play.

There are a great many wonderful days that we get to celebrate together with our spouses. There are a great many challenging and difficult days where we need to support each other. As good and hard seasons come and go, we learn to rely on each other, support each other, and grow closer together. We recognize that the hard times actually forge our bonds even closer together then when it's always sunshine and rainbows.

Can we make a commitment to restore the covenant of marriage to its rightful place of being a good thing? I'm afraid our culture has dimmed its appeal. May we all shine a bright light from our God-honoring, Christian foundation marriage to others to encourage them that God's blessing indeed shines out from our homes because our hearts are properly aligned with His!

Lord, we thank you for the favor you shine on our lives.
May we honor you in our marriages and in our homes.

Design Tip

Don't worry if you don't have a lot of seasonal decorations. Many things can be made into seasonal decor. Take time to think of what you and your new spouse think of when fall and Christmas and summer come around rather than seeing what Target has on their shelf.

PAIGE RIEN

Showing Honor

Likewise, husbands, live with your wives in an understanding way,
showing honor to the woman as the weaker vessel, since they are heirs
with you of the grace of life, so that your prayers may not be hindered.

I Peter 3:7 ESV

While this verse specifically addresses husbands, I love the application for all of us here. "Live in an understanding way." So good, right? Living with understanding can prove challenging as two lives merge into one. Perhaps part of the challenge revolves around the fact that having understanding requires a listening ear, a loving tone and a pleasant demeanor.

Living in an understanding way with one another stewards our relationship on a good path and a harmonious marriage brings glory to God. An effective practice of listening to understand is vital to maintaining a clear and good relationship with one another. We accomplish this by being sure to hear what's being said. By working to understand when our spouse is saying something important. Speaking in a tender tone with grace filled words, seasoned with salt takes practice. A pleasant demeanor when we've had a bad day or are frustrated can be the very last thing, we want to give to each other. And yet that is living in an understanding way.

When we put into practice these relationship-building skills, we see the benefits of God's blessing on our lives.

Father, help me learn what it really means to live in an understanding way.
Help me pursue peace in my relationship today!

Love Is. . .

Charity suffereth long, and is kind; charity envieth not; charity vaunteth not itself,
is not puffed up, Doth not behave itself unseemly, seeketh not her own, is not easily provoked,
thinketh no evil; Rejoiceth not in iniquity, but rejoiceth in the truth; Beareth all things,
believeth all things, hopeth all things, endureth all things. Charity never faileth.

I Corinthians 13:4–8a KJV

The books and movies never show the whole picture, do they? Happily ever after in two hours or less creates unhealthy expectations! Instead, a relationship of love that lasts a lifetime will be built on a different foundation. Feelings ebb and flow based on the events of the day, the stress of jobs, family and finances. But love that lasts learns to be patient and kind. A love that lasts learns not to be selfish or cranky.

True love bears a lot—offering to each other the same grace upon grace as our Father has given us. We believe and hope and endure because love never ends. We are shown the best example of love in how Jesus loves us all throughout the pages of Scripture. No matter what happens, His love never fails us. Ever.

This kind of love provides security. When we argue, disagree, or become frustrated, my husband and I have committed to not only stay up until we talk through our issues—which makes for late nights sometimes—but we also committed to not threatening to file for divorce. This commitment protects the space for us to communicate and express ourselves while providing security of a safe space. Can I encourage you to make the same pact with your spouse? After twenty-five years of marriage, I know that this has been crucial to our foundation. We are far from perfect, but we trust our perfect Father to continue to draw us closer to Him and to each other.

Marriage Tip

Pray and read the Bible together.

NAOMI MCINTOSH

Forgiveness

For if you forgive other people when they sin against you, your heavenly Father will also forgive you. But if you do not forgive others their sins, your Father will not forgive your sins.

MATTHEW 6:14–15 NIV

One of the best things you can do for your marriage is to keep an attitude of forgiveness in your home. We are all fallible and even if they do things unintentionally, we may still be hurt by our spouse.

While we might wish to withhold that forgiveness, doing so puts us at odds with God and will yield separation in our relationship instead of growing closer with both God and our husband. Being quick to offer an apology when we are in the wrong and offering forgiveness freely without restitution is important. We forgive not only because it keeps our relationship strong, but also because the Lord commands it of us. We cannot harbor unforgiveness in our hearts and expect to have a right relationship with God.

We are a people forgiven of much—our debts are incalculable against our holy God. As a person who has been forgiven over and over again freely and without question, we are to offer the same forgiveness to our spouse. Being intentional to practice forgiveness regularly will help us remain on the right side of our relationships, both with God and our husbands.

Lord, give me the understanding and strength to practice giving forgiveness regularly and faithfully to my husband. Thank you for the forgiveness you've shown me when I've failed you!

Marriage Tip

Communicate problem issues quickly. Don't give Satan any space in your relationship to stir up anger and resentment.

JENNIFER INGRAM

Seek Him First

But seek first the kingdom of God and his righteousness, and all these things
will be added to you. Therefore do not be anxious about tomorrow,
for tomorrow will be anxious for itself. Sufficient for the day is its own trouble.

Matthew 6:33–34 ESV

One of the keys to living the Christian life well and partnering in marriage well is to seek God first. Keeping God as the center of your relationship is essential to honoring him and keeping him as our priority. When Christ is the center, our home becomes a much happier place to be and honors God.

An added benefit of keeping Christ as the center of our marriage is that we also acknowledge that all we have is a gift from above. We don't have to live with anxious fear of what tomorrow holds. We rest in Him because He has our lives in his hands. He is sufficient and supreme and sovereign over all. This brings us abundant peace as we walk the path He has chosen for us together. We can have confidence that He has us right where He wants us, and we can walk ahead with the peace of that knowledge.

The beauty of seeking Him first together in our marriage is that as we grow closer to God, we also grow closer to each other. When our hearts are aligned with God's, we will also find as a benefit that our hearts are more aligned with each other.

Thank you, Lord, for the reminder today to seek you first! Help us to continue to seek you
as we continue to work together building a strong foundation for our marriage.

Marriage Tip
Always
choose love.
Believe the best
in your spouse.
And choose love.

Nagging

Better to live on a corner of the roof than share a house with a quarrelsome wife.
PROVERBS 21:9 NIV

Can you imagine with me for a moment someone preferring to stay in the corner of a large house because it's more peaceful, or quiet, or less stressful there? I realize it seems a bit of stretch, but how many times do we retreat into quieter rooms, behind closed doors, away from the stress and strain? How many times does our spouse do the same, preferring to work late hours, or hide in plain sight to play video games, watch tv, decompress?

None of those things are wrong, mind you, and many of us introverts need our space and quiet while the extroverts love to visit! But if our husbands are hiding because we are nagging them, perhaps we should reconsider our actions. Many times, my words are impossible to move my husband to action. In fact, I often use too many words! The truth is I need to speak my piece in love and gentleness, and if a disagreement still occurs, I need to remove my words and my thoughts from the conversation and go to the Lord with my concerns.

Obviously the bigger the argument, the harder this is to do. In my own power, I want to advocate why I'm right and why he's wrong, but the truth is eventually my words sound like "blah, blah, blah" and does zero to help me with my cause. In reality, going to the Lord is my greatest strategy because the Lord will either change my heart to align with my husbands, or I learn to trust that He will work in my husband for His purpose.

*Father help me to purpose to cultivate a place of peace for our home
by removing the natural inclination I have to nag!*

Design Tip

When you're styling
a shelf, coffee table,
or console table always
think in terms of using
items in odd numbers.
For example, using
3, 5, or 7 candlesticks
is much more pleasing
to the eye than 2, 4, or 6.

JENNIFER INGRAM

Listen Up

Listen to advice and accept instruction, that you may gain wisdom in the future.
PROVERBS 19:20 ESV

Some of us struggle more than others. Some of us seek advice easily, and some of us don't. We feel this innate pressure to figure it out on our own by trial and error, learning as we go.

If you couldn't tell, I definitely fall into this category. It would be far better for me to seek instruction and be wise, but instead I try very hard to find the information on my own. Sometimes this listening that I need to do comes into play with my husband. Instead of trying to come up with solutions to the budget, the laundry, or even the dinner plans on my own all the time, it would be so much better and wiser to seek him out to find out what his thoughts and plans are. Can you relate?

It's easy to move through life independently, and while this can be very healthy when kept in balance, it can quickly become unmanageable when it isn't. A healthy balance means asking others for their advice and instruction. A mentor, a couple who has been married for many years, a husband, a friend can all offer helpful advice in the days ahead. Don't be afraid to utilize their instruction and gain wisdom!

Learning to bear one another's burdens isn't just about helping everyone else. Sometimes it's about allowing others to do what they do well and take the pressure off our shoulders. How many blessings do we prevent others from receiving because we are unwilling to accept help when we need it?

Dear Father, help me to remember that needing help isn't a liability or a flaw. Remind me of the importance of seeking help regularly.

Marriage Tip

Celebrate all the wins
with your spouse—
big and small,
make it a habit
to celebrate.

Lord, help me to
learn to choose my
battles wisely,
to stay on target,
and to choose to
let go when it's over.
Give me wisdom
to navigate these
difficult waters.

Fuel for the Fire

For lack of wood the fire goes out, and where there is no whisperer, quarreling ceases.
PROVERBS 26:20 ESV

In order for an argument to go from a low burn to an all-out forest fire it requires a source to keep feeding on. Now in my twenty-five years of marriage there has been no lack in the number of times I've brought plenty of kindling to throw on that fire. I don't say that with pride, but rather in an effort to be transparent. Instead of being a voice of an expert, I want you to know that I struggle with the same things you do.

An argument gets derailed off topic when we interject universal statements like "You never. . ." or "You always. . ." You get the idea. It's really easy to veer off the topic at hand when you are upset, hurt, or frustrated. The key to successfully navigating the waters of conflict is to stay on topic. Don't be tempted to reinforce your feelings and thoughts by attacking the person or their faults. It's so easy to do, friend, but restrain yourself. Stick to the matter at hand and work through it. And when it's over let the flame die.

I'm one who has my best arguments after they are over. I have to sit and think and sort through my thoughts. This usually occurs the next day or in the shower. I can deliberate and ruminate on what I should have said. I have found though that this is an absolutely terrible trait. Instead of letting it go and letting the fire burn out, thinking about what I should have said only makes the argument flare up again. I have to be intentional to not allow myself to brood on the things I should have or could have said. Be careful how long you sit with your feelings, friends! Better to let go and move on to continue to pursue the peace that you desire in your home.

Marriage Tip

Text for no reason.

NAOMI MCINTOSH

The Problem
with Abraham and Isaac

When the men of the place asked him [Isaac] about his wife, he said,
"She is my sister," for he feared to say, "My wife," thinking, "lest the men of the place
should kill me because of Rebekah," because she was attractive in appearance.

GENESIS 26:7 ESV

ometimes history repeats itself. This may be a strange passage for us to consider, however, I wanted to address the problem that deceit brings in marriages. I am surprised at how Isaac handles this particular situation. His own mother and father experienced the same fear and the same course of action when Abraham lied to the king, saying he was Sarah's brother.

You would think that this would have been a teachable opportunity for Abraham to share with his son. And this isn't the only issue. Isaac had the opportunity to teach his sons the lessons he had learned, but instead the deceitfulness continued as he was deceived by Rebekah when Jacob received his father's blessing instead of Esau. A heritage of deceit rooted in fear and doubt of God's hand of blessing to provide. Ouch.

Now obviously none of this derailed God's plans for them, or for the people of Israel, yet the angst, doubt, and hurt present in these situations could have been prevented. Many times, we are devastated when we don't learn lessons from the past. May we be faithful to root out the default nature of deceit in our hearts. May we be diligent to trust God's plan in our own lives and in our marriages.

Lord, help me faithfully root out this deceit that can
run rampant in our lives and through generations.

Perfect Harmony

And above all these put on love, which binds everything together in perfect harmony.
COLOSSIANS 3:14 ESV

This passage gives us a great list of the behaviors or attributes that set us apart as God's people. Compassionate hearts, kindness, patience, and forgiveness, color these verses that conclude with the encouragement to be a people known by our love because love brings harmony.

As a musician I love the reference here of perfect harmony. You can have a strong melody, interesting rhythms, and even gorgeous lyrics, however, harmony is the stuff of texture and beauty that fills out the spaces, drawing attention to the melody in all the right ways.

A harmonious relationship filled with love for one another means our beautiful melody—Christ—is being given the attention and adoration He deserves. He alone is worthy. Because a peaceful and loving relationship looks so different to our culture today, this harmony can be a catalyst to bring God glory through our marriage. To understand that loving my husband well brings harmony and peace in my home is just one piece that draws others to also experience Christ's love and is a wonderful reminder of the Great Commission today.

*Dear Lord, I pray that you will use my marriage even today
to bring you glory and draw others to your saving grace!
Thank you for the opportunity to be a part of the work you are doing.*

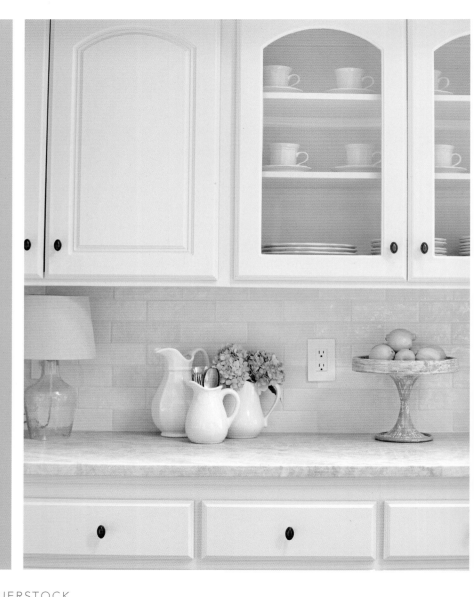

Marriage Tip

Be patient in the process. Merging two lives together takes time and getting the silverware in the drawers, and the sheets and towels in the cabinets requires patience and flexibility.

Three-Fold Cord

And though a man might prevail against one who is alone,
two will withstand him—a threefold cord is not quickly broken.

<small>ECCLESIASTES 4:12 ESV</small>

This verse is personally meaningful because it was read at our wedding ceremony twenty-five years ago. One of our pastors illustrated this verse in Ecclesiastes with a piece of rope to tie a knot during his address to us as newlyweds.

The piece of three-fold cord or rope was such a strong visual example for us. We each come as one part of the rope in this marriage covenant. We each bring our strengths and weaknesses together, knowing that in joining together we are stronger. Better together than apart. The key is to strengthen our union even further. With Christ as the focal point, the center, the third piece of rope joined with us can form a bond that cannot be broken. Sharing a common love for our Savior, drawing ever closer to him day after day, year after year, we bond more to each other as well. And that bond is something that can face the daily grind, the hurts, habits, and hang-ups of the challenges we face in our lives.

Friends, don't forget the power of God in the middle of our union. He is the bond that can hold us together through whatever storm we face.

I thank you, dear Lord, for being the strength in our rope.
Being stronger together is a great reminder to remain grounded in your truth.

Design Tip

Remember you can add knobs or change hardware on any furniture to make it more "you." This is a nice way to balance masculine and feminine.

PAIGE RIEN

Kindness

And be ye kind one to another, tenderhearted, forgiving one another,
even as God for Christ's sake hath forgiven you.
EPHESIANS 4:32 KJV

Have you noticed a tendency to treat those closest to you with a little less than love and kindness? It's true that being comfortable with a relationship is appealing because when we are tired, stressed, or cranky, we can be real and open and honest. And sometimes when we are that way, our words and actions are the opposite of kindness.

Speaking and acting in kindness with a tender heart requires intention and purpose. Sometimes it means biting my tongue figuratively and literally! I certainly don't like being unappreciated or talked to unkindly, so why would I want to saddle my partner with that kind of treatment?

I think I especially noticed my tendency to constant sarcastic talk—which was funny, I thought, until it was coming out of the mouth of my toddler. Instead of sounding funny, it sounded rude, belittling, and unkind. When I wanted to scold her, I realized I had no one to blame but myself. Kids repeat what they hear. Her words sounded so harsh in my ears, it caused me to re-assess how I spoke to my husband!

Be cautious, sweet friend—use words of kindness, tones of gentleness, and be appealing in our speech and actions to our husbands. Don't treat strangers better. That's just not kind.

Lord, move my lips to speak with gracious talk, encouragement,
and a tone that conveys an attitude of love to my spouse.

Marriage Tip

Leave sweet
or encouraging
notes in places
they'll find them.

NAOMI MCINTOSH

Bond of Peace

With all humility and gentleness, with patience, bearing with one another in love,
eager to maintain the unity of the Spirit in the bond of peace.
EPHESIANS 4:2–3 ESV

Sometimes the Bible can be just so stunning in its clarity. Sometimes we hold out understanding the Bible as something so mysterious and hard to grasp. The reality is that so much of the Bible is straight talk and maybe just maybe we don't like to hear what it has to say.

What I mean is this. Our passage today is quite plain—a recipe of sorts. Generous helpings of humility and gentleness, a dash of patience and a heaping cupfull of love create the recipe of unity in a bond of peace.

Peace is so needed in our homes and in our world. So many people are longing and looking for peace and we have just the right recipe in front of us. Practicing humility and gentleness with our spouse should be intentional. Having a love filled with patience should be our daily activity.

So many times, we want deeper meaning, a checklist, or creative infographic, and those are a great source of help; however, if we also apply the truth of God's Word to our hearts and our homes, we will see an abundant harvest.

Be humble and gentle. Learn to be patient and long suffering through love. Be eager to unify in the Spirit. Peace is the fruit of a love crop well planted and nurtured.

Lord, help me to remember to keep it simple—do what you've asked,
obey what the Bible teaches, and allow you to bless with a harvest of peace.

Marriage Tip

Keep Christ at the center. You don't have to have a cross over your bed if you don't want to— but find ways to keep Him at the center of your marriage. He is in it with you.

PAIGE RIEN

Help Meet

And the LORD God said, It is not good that the man should be alone;
I will make him an help meet for him.

GENESIS 2:18 KJV

Reading through the Creation story is awe inspiring. I am awed by so many facets of creation from the land and water, to the sun and stars, to the animals and Adam. The vision God had as Creator is far beyond my understanding. He made it all perfectly. After God created man, He recognized, man needed woman. This is a beautiful part of the story for me.

Throughout history women have not always been treated well solely because of their gender. Less than. Unnecessary. Unwanted. I have had my own moments where I have been dismissed or disregarded because of my femininity. God corrects this viewpoint here in this passage. God declares that because man should not be alone, our role is neither doormat nor ruler but right beside him, helping. Man needed woman as the perfect helper for him.

Without the introduction of sin into this perfect relationship, our relationships today would likely be much more peaceful naturally. In marriage, we are equal partners with different roles. Not everyone's marriage looks the same because we are all unique. As women, we can value our role as helpers for our husbands because that's exactly how God designed us to be. And our husband will value us being the helper he needs to do all that God has created him to do.

Gracious Father, thank you for designing us with just the unique capabilities
to serve each other together. Help me to see my value and do all to fulfill
this special calling you've placed on my life.

Marriage Tip

Make sure to take time to learn new things together. This can be a hobby, a sport or training or a fun side hustle.

Gongs and Cymbals

If I speak in the tongues of men and of angels, but have not love, I am a noisy gong or a clanging cymbal. And if I have prophetic powers, and understand all mysteries and all knowledge, and if I have all faith, so as to remove mountains, but have not love, I am nothing. If I give away all I have, and if I deliver up my body to be burned, but have not love, I gain nothing.

I Corinthians 13:1–3 ESV

This entire chapter is one of my favorites in the Bible. It was read at our wedding while we lit our unity candle. It is so descriptive and visual for me.

I can speak with amazing words and wow an audience, but if I lack love, I'm just a noisy gong or a terrible cymbal crash. I can predict the future, unravel mystery with my knowledge, be wise beyond my years, and even move a mountain with my faith but lack love in my interactions with others, then these noble things are worth nothing. If I gave all my possessions away and sacrificed myself as a martyr without loving people as God loves them, then the sacrifice is worth nothing in the end.

Sacrifice without love is not enough. Knowledge and wisdom without love is empty. Powerful speech and motivation and large crowds are meaningless.

This love chapter adjures us to love one another because the greatest of these—faith, hope and love—is love. In our marriages may we not work to be the most knowledgeable, the best dressed and well-spoken or the most sacrificial without also doing the work of being loving. In the end nothing matters if we don't love well.

Say the words. Do the actions. Be love. Be different.

God, grant me the ability to love well. Fill me with your spirit and power to communicate love and care to my husband.

Love in Action

Let all that you do be done in love.
I Corinthians 16:14 ESV

While this may seem to be a pretty simple verse, we must acknowledge it's not a simple verse to put into action. The challenge here lies in not just reading the verse and agreeing with the principle, but actually moving forward and acting upon it all.

And there's that pesky little word all. It's all inclusive and overwhelming. It's complete in its entirety and proves once again that love is a priority in our marriage relationship. Every single thing in this life that we do, should be wrapped up and carried in love. The presentation is with love, the action is done because of love, and our husbands should receive the love we give them in the end.

What a beautiful picture of how things should really work! How much of a difference could we make in this world with this principle behind our every action within our marriage? How much more could our marriages be places of comfort and joy if we behaved in such a way as to live this truth out each and every day?

Let's live with love as our focus as we go through our daily routines. Remember the reason that love reigns supreme is because God is love!

I pray, dear Father, that you will continue to fill me with your Holy Spirit power to love as you do and to communicate love in all of my actions.

Design Tip

Keep an eye out for furniture with storage options. These are great for storing extra items out of sight and keeping your space clutter free. Ottomans, benches, and baskets are great choices to use for your extra stuff.

God Is Love

No man hath seen God at any time.
If we love one another, God dwelleth in us, and his love is perfected in us.

I John 4:12 KJV

In the process of joining our lives together as one, we must merge not just the pillows and the blankets, but our entire way of doing things. How we fold the towels, load the dishwasher, and squeeze the toothpaste, just to name a few! We find all of the quirks in this process of uniting our home cute—until they become annoying.

Part of the merging process requires bringing God into the very center of our lives each and every day. The intentional focused effort will prove to be essential to us because He is love. When we learn to care for and love each other the way that God loves, then we can live in such a way that others will see God at work in us. Because no one has seen God, a faithless world can only "see" him through our lives. When our lives overflow with love for each other, we can then demonstrate how important it is that they know and understand that God is love.

Practicing this type of love requires surrender on our part.

Surrender to doing God's will instead of our own.

Surrender to the Holy Spirit's leading and direction in my life.

Surrender to the perfect sovereign plan that God has for us.

Lord, help me to remember to surrender my way to yours.
Remind me that this is the way to true happiness and joy.

Marriage Tip

Make time for each other. Put down the phones. Mute the TV and look each other in the eyes.

❧

Make me vigilant, dear Lord, to protect the boundaries of my marriage. Help me to remember that joy is rooted in you and to trust your plan.

True Commitment

So guard yourselves in your spirit, and let none of you be faithless to the wife of your youth.
MALACHI 2:15B ESV

Tackling the importance of commitment in our relationships is challenging. It is almost easier to talk about love, kindness, gentleness, and peace on the pages of this book. These are the happy things of marriage and the spirit with which we entered our sacred union together in those first days. Although I'd rather talk about the positive attributes of love and care for one another, it would be a complete miss if I didn't offer a word of warning about some of the things that can creep in when you least expect them. Being truly committed to your marriage relationship is an important act of obedience and faithfulness.

Whether it's an old boyfriend or a comfortable work relationship, sometimes feelings pop up that we feel are justified. I can't tell you how many times I've heard that God wants us to be happy. While I do believe that God desires that we be filled with joy here on this earth, we must also recognize that we will not always be happy. And there is no requirement that marriage should make me happy.

We must always be on guard and vigilant to keep the boundaries of our marriage securely established and firm. We must remove any source of temptation in our life so that we don't fail to be anything less than completely faithful in our marriage. This might mean unfriending someone on social media or blocking an email address or phone number. It might mean moving a desk at work or changing your shift. Can I encourage you to take action to put your guard up? Being proactive to stop any plan of the devil to get a foothold in your relationship is so incredibly important to be truly committed in your marriage relationship.

Marriage Tip

Make their favorite cool, fun dinners regularly!
Remember to keep the pantry or fridge stocked with their favorite foods and snacks.

NAOMI MCINTOSH

One Flesh

"But from the beginning of creation, 'God made them male and female.'
'Therefore, a man shall leave his father and mother and hold fast to his wife,
and the two shall become one flesh.' So they are no longer two but one flesh.
What therefore God has joined together, let not man separate."

MARK 10:6–9 ESV

These are the very words spoken by Jesus reminding us of the truth from the dawn of Creation recorded for us in the book of Genesis. God created a helpmeet named Eve for Adam and declared that they were no longer two separate people but one flesh in the bonds of marriage.

In a marriage partnership we have rewritten the operating agreement. Instead of being individually responsible for decisions and judgment calls about everything from what to eat for dinner to what time to go to bed, we now have another person in the mix. This uniting process is not always simple, but it is necessary. God wanted us to no longer be separate entities living under the same roof, rather we are to merge our lives and become one new person.

This is an important distinction for us to remember. Some of us are solo operators and are quite capable of decision making, handling problems and creating solutions all on our own. But we are no longer on a solo mission and we shouldn't behave that way any longer. Because God has joined us together, we should walk out the truth of the Gospel together. Being united means having the same purpose and goals as a couple. We never lose our identity in this process, rather, we find balance and strength in becoming one flesh.

Lord, continue molding and making me into the person you desire me to be. Help me to continue merging my life with my husbands in order to most effectively serve you together.

Keep scripture in front of you, always. And change it up as you go, preferably from your Bible—not in a premade sign—because this means you had contact with His word in the Bible and that verse is meant for you. Letter boards are truly designed for this.

PAIGE RIEN

Love and Faithfulness

Let not steadfast love and faithfulness forsake you; bind them around your neck;
write them on the tablet of your heart. So you will find favor
and good success in the sight of God and man.

PROVERBS 3:3–4 ESV

Like a horse and carriage or peanut butter and jelly, Proverbs reminds us that love and faithfulness are equal partners. Love and faithfulness bring favor with God and man and set up our marriages for great success. Loving each other well and being faithful are the cornerstones of building your life on a sure foundation.

Steadfast love is unmovable. Though winds of change, discontentment, and dissatisfaction come and go, a steadfast love doesn't get blown off course. Faithfulness is an added component of this steadfast love because it doesn't wander. It doesn't get restless. It doesn't need to always be built up. Steadfast love just is.

Often, we see the lack of faithfulness and steadfastness in marriages in our world today. It's a sad and sorrowful thing for us to miss out on the beauty of this kind of love because we don't have any idea what it means to be steadfast or unmovable. My prayer for you is that you will discover how rich and lovely a steadfast love is and can be in your marriage and that you will not long for something else that will only leave you desperate for a real and true and deep love.

Lord, I thank you for the reminder today that a steadfast love is made stronger
with faithfulness. May I always love my husband in this manner!

Marriage Tip

Don't keep score.
If you do, you'll never
be happy. Life isn't fair.
Marriage is like life.

JULIE LANCIA

One Up on You

Let love be genuine. Abhor what is evil; hold fast to what is good.
Love one another with brotherly affection. Outdo one another in showing honor.
ROMANS 12:9–10 ESV

Listed as marks of the Christian, I believe that all believers need to put into practice these truths in their everyday lives. Beyond this, I believe there is a distinct application within the bond of marriage to benefit from.

Sometimes we might go through the motions of showing love to our spouse or work to feel our spouse's love on some days. And yet it's easy to spot genuine love. With genuine love, we know there is no desire for our own benefit. We love because we hold on to what we know is good and righteous. This allows love to grow and flourish.

When we are truly affectionate with one another, we treat each other with gentleness and kindness because we want our spouse to have the best. But perhaps my favorite words of all come at the end of these verses: "outdo one another in showing honor." Those of us who are competitive by nature know what it's like to outdo one another. It's the nature of the competition to win.

What if we turned that same intensity in trying to outdo each other in demonstrating love and honor and respect? Can you imagine what our homes might look and feel like? When we treat others better than ourselves, we put our own self-interests aside and seek only what's best for our spouse. It's a beautiful picture that each of us get to take part in.

Father, show me how to continue to demonstrate love in my home.
Help me to learn how to best outdo my husband in demonstrating love, honor, and respect.

Marriage Tip

Seek pre-marital counseling from your church home. It's a wonderful way to build a strong foundation from the early days of your marriage.

JENNIFER INGRAM

Loving Well

Owe no man any thing, but to love one another: for he that loveth another hath fulfilled
the law. For this, Thou shalt not commit adultery, Thou shalt not kill, Thou shalt not steal,
Thou shalt not bear false witness, Thou shalt not covet; and if there be any other commandment,
it is briefly comprehended in this saying, namely, Thou shalt love thy neighbour as thyself.
Love worketh no ill to his neighbour: therefore love is the fulfilling of the law.

ROMANS 13:8–10 KJV

Talking about the law and obedience seems possibly a little off topic. But I'd like to posit this—we are commanded to love, and we are expected to obey the laws that God has given us. Therefore, fulfilling the law by loving well is being obedient!

Verse nine is clear. The Ten Commandments included the warnings to not commit adultery, to not murder or steal or covet, and the New Testament summed up our job as believers to love your neighbor as yourself.

Verse ten concludes that because we are told to love our neighbor then loving each other helps us keep the other commands. Because let's be honest: we will not be seeking a relationship outside of our marriage if we are committed to loving each other well through good times and bad.

Time and time again, we are given an emphasis on love. Not because it's a happy feeling or just a squishy emotion. Rather, it's the root—the sturdy, strong foundation of building a life together. It's the intention of pursuing love in our relationship that will set us up to share a lifetime of memories together.

Father, thank you for the truth of your word to guide us
and help us build the strong foundation we need for our future.

Just One Look

You have captivated my heart, my sister, my bride; you have captivated my heart with one glance of your eyes, with one jewel of your necklace.
SONG OF SOLOMON 4:9 ESV

Solomon sure had a way with words, didn't he? Song of Solomon is quite descriptive with a lot of verses we could turn to as we look at our marriages through the lens of God's Word.

This particular verse grabs my attention in the way it describes the loving look we give, "one glance of your eyes." When we want to captivate a man's attention early on, we ladies know what look to give! We know how powerful that glance can be, the look that says we are interested or intrigued by this man.

But somewhere along the way, it's easy to stop looking our men in the eyes or giving them the approval and appreciation they deserve and that captivates their hearts. It might seem silly, but I do think that when we have held on to certain hurts or long days and even longer nights with the babies in tow, we forget to make the men in our lives still feel needed and important. A quick glance, the moment of acknowledgement can help us stay connected even in the midst of these seasons. Don't forget how powerful it is to be seen and known—and make sure we offer this grace to our husbands as well.

Father, thank you that you see us and know us in the midst of it all.
Help us to communicate love to our husbands in not just word
or actions but also in the glances we give them!

Laugh.
Laughter is like
oxygen to
a marriage.
We have to make
each other laugh.
And we have to
laugh at ourselves.
We have to infuse
every day with joy.
When we infuse
lightheartedness
into our days
they don't seem
as hard.

JULIE LANCIA

Two Are Better

Two are better than one, because they have a good return for their labor.
ECCLESIASTES 4:9 NIV

Any task that needs doing always gets done more quickly when more people get involved. It doesn't matter what it is, many hands make light work. The same is true in our marriages. When we are working together toward a common goal, we will not only be much happier, but we will also get more done. When our relationships are in the right place, we can do more kingdom work because we are not distracted by a dysfunctional relationship.

Working together creates its own chaos though. We are human after all. I have worked on and off for my husband throughout the years. This can create friction. He has a way he likes to operate—he is a first born after all. I have a way I like to operate—I am an only child. So, you can imagine that our preferences for the way to work, and what we believe is important or essential probably varies. We have completely different points of view on just about everything and this can easily create frustration and annoyance. We have to work together to understand and be flexible.

Flexibility happens over time. This is the nice part about being a few years down the road together. We start to expect that what we want to do or what we are valuing in the moment might need to be adjusted to match our partner's vision. We learn to appreciate the difference in perspective because it actually brings richness to our lives. Remember, you gain strength by having your husband on your team as you both work together!

Father, we thank you for bringing our marriage together
and helping us work toward a common goal together!

Lord, help me to leave it all in your hands. Help me to make it my habit to turn to you in prayer first over any and all frustrations.

Submission

Submitting yourselves one to another in the fear of God.

EPHESIANS 5:21 KJV

Submission is not a well-received topic in today's day and age. As a matter of fact, it's largely taboo to even talk about vows in a marriage ceremony, including the traditional "love, honor, and obey" for women.

I believe that Ephesians adds another layer for us to consider as it teaches us to submit to one another out of the reverence we have for Christ. In our marriages, submission is not often understood as an intentional act. There are times where disagreements make the idea of submission harder to stomach. This is where we have a decision to make.

What happens when we don't want to submit? We pray. Rather than cajole or try various means of manipulation in our marriages, can I encourage you instead to take it to God in prayer?

When we feel powerless—pray.

When we feel helpless—pray.

When we are angry—pray.

When we are frustrated—pray.

When we are wrong—pray.

When we are right—pray.

I mean it—when the decision has been made and you don't think it's right, go pray about it until you are done wrestling. Turning it over to God is the very best thing you can do for yourself and for your marriage to be peaceful and harmonious.

Keep memories close—display your family pictures!
Find ways to create cozy corners,
or a gallery wall with your favorite memories.

Multiplication

So God created man in his own image, in the image of God he created him; male and female
he created them. And God blessed them. And God said to them, "Be fruitful and multiply
and fill the earth and subdue it and have dominion over the fish of the sea
and over the birds of the heavens and over every living thing that moves on the earth."
GENESIS 1:27–28 ESV

From the beginning of the Creation story, we see God's plan for our marriages. Male and female created in God's own image. God blessed the marriage union in the garden at the beginning of our time on earth and followed it with the command to be fruitful and multiply, to fill the earth with all humanity, and to be above the fish, birds, and other animals that were also created.

Man was set apart because he was created by God in His image. The animals and the rest of creation cannot claim the same. The command to be fruitful and multiply launched the human race and even though God knew in advance that sin would enter the garden and damage his perfect plan for all mankind, He did it anyway.

The devastation of sin in the garden and in our lives even now makes the marriage union more work than God ever intended. But two partners devoted to each other and to doing the work of pursuing peace in their marriage is the most beautiful picture of God's purpose in our marriages!

Father, I thank you that you don't give up on us ever, and that you love us unwaveringly!
Help me show the same kind of love in my marriage.

Marriage Tip

Never hide your spending from each other.
Don't hide the packages that get delivered.
Be honest and open—you'll never regret it.

Faith, Hope, and Love

So now faith, hope, and love abide, these three; but the greatest of these is love.
I Corinthians 13:13 ESV

Within our marriages I hope we all find faith, hope, and love. I'm writing this particular volume during a season with little faith, hope, or love in our culture. It's difficult to watch just how divided and isolated we have become, but I pray for us to cultivate more connection and community inside the walls of our homes. And when we have this place, our homes, secure and whole, my prayer is that a watching world can observe the power of Christ at the center of our marriage with faith hope and love at its core.

Some days are easier than others. I have often said if I lived on top of a mountain without people, I sure could be a much nicer, holier, sweeter, and kinder person! But not only is this unrealistic, it's also very unnatural. We were created to live in community, therefore, our marriages can and should reflect the power we have in Christ.

Unfortunately, too many times we turn the TV on, scroll the socials, burn the bread, and squeeze the toothpaste in the middle of the tube. We let the little frustrations and the annoyances of what we believe is wrong in the world invade our space and affect our interactions with one another.

Working to respond to each other within the boundaries of faith, hope, and love can give us an opportunity to be salt and light in ways we've not seen possible before. But we have to work at it and be responsible to weed out the nastiness that tries to steal away our faith, hope, and love.

Fill me with faith, hope, and love Lord so that I may overflow in my home and in my community!

Marriage Tip

Plan adventures.
Having something
exciting to look
forward to
is always fun!

Abide in Love

So we have come to know and to believe the love that God has for us.
God is love, and whoever abides in love abides in God, and God abides in him.

I JOHN 4:16 ESV

Abiding and dwelling. Interesting thoughts from Scripture that make me think of our homes—our dwelling places. I also love to investigate when a verse begins with the word "so." Beginning with the word "so" means that there is added context behind the verses we are reading, which makes me look back at previous verses to know more about what's going on here. The verses that precede this passage indicate that when Christ lives in us, we recognize the goodness of God and His love to us. We abide in him and He in us.

This abiding proves to us the existence of not only His love for us—all mankind—but also His great love to us personally. And here's the ultimate reality. Because His love lives in us, we can in turn love each other well. His love through us means we are the conduits. It's a beautiful picture really, because if left to my own devices, I'm selfish, cranky, and completely unlovable. Yet when I allow the power of Christ to live in me as I'm abiding and dwelling with Him and He with me—well then, it's game on! I have the power I need to love my spouse no matter the circumstances happening around me.

I am so grateful for that power Lord! May I always be filled with your Spirit
and connected to that source of strength because I'm abiding and dwelling with you!

Design Tip

You can make a fancy tablescape with what you have. One of my favorite tricks is using a few yards of fabric as a runner, bunched up if you hate to iron.

PAIGE RIEN

Earnest Love

Above all, love each other deeply, because love covers over a multitude of sins.
I Peter 4:8 NIV

Here again we find instructions to the church or Christians in general. The reality is that this truth applied to our marriages will really make such a difference in our lives.

When I love earnestly, it's not haphazard or occasionally. It's not love because I feel loved but rather because I love no matter how I feel, how I have been treated, or any other things I may add as limitations to my obedience to love.

An earnest love isn't concerned with the rules of the strict definition of love. Loving earnestly might even mean being hurt or having ourselves exposed and vulnerable. Instead, it's like the athlete who leaves it all on the field the day of play. It's an all-or-nothing gift with no expectations or strings attached.

But love also covers a multitude of sins. I like to think of this as the relationship that loves no matter what. No matter the tense words, forgotten special days or seasons of distance, love continues to show up. Love shows up in our aging and change. Love covers up by offering grace when we aren't the best versions of our selves. No matter the changes through the years, I can return that love to my husband with a richness and deepness forged in a gift of truth that binds my heart to my spouse.

I would never trade that kind of love for a superficial and meaningless substitute. Give me real, lasting, and enduring love any day.

Lord, I praise you for the gift of an earnest and enduring love. Thank you for the example you've given us in your Word of what that kind of love looks like!

Marriage Tip

Surprise your spouse
with treats or gifts
that they like.

NAOMI MCINTOSH

. . . and Is Kind

Love suffers long and is kind.
I Corinthians 13:4 ESV

I've memorized this passage before and even contemplated its meaning before. But only recently have I thought of the importance of the word "and" between the two thoughts of love: suffering long and love is kind.

Though we understand that loving our spouse requires longsuffering and we practice loving kindly, pairing them together might present a little different connotation. When I am longsuffering with someone, especially my husband, it might also include a bit of impatience, frustration, or eye rolling. I am living out the letter of the law without really understanding the spirit involved. The Pharisees were awfully good at that and Jesus called them out for it.

See He doesn't want us to be rule followers for the sake of the rules themselves, rather He longs for our hearts! In the same way, our hearts will love each other differently when we understand that loving well includes additional fruits of the spirit. Kindness is that extra special touch that makes the love feel even stronger and more meaningful.

The reality is that adding in "and is kind" displays an extra distinction to our longsuffering and our love. This will make us behave much differently when we are trying to love each other well.

Father, help me learn to love with both longsuffering and kindness,
so that I may more fully express the kind of long-lasting love you have given to us.

Divorce should never be an option, discussion, or exit strategy. Marriage is "until death parts us." Focus on the ultimate goal of helping each other get to Heaven.

JENNIFER INGRAM

Love Like Jesus

This is my commandment, That ye love one another, as I have loved you.
JOHN 15:12 KJV

At the end of the day, no matter what we face, we can demonstrate God's love to others, by loving each other well. I believe our marriages can be a declaration of the beauty of the Gospel to a world in need of this truth today.

We declare His Word to be true by living it out in our homes and with each other. When we love each other in our homes the way Jesus loves us, there can be no misunderstanding or confusion about where our allegiance lies.

When the world around is quick to dissolve the less than perfect unions, we continue to love just like Jesus loves us.

We continue to love no matter the illness, the debt, the trials. In this way we reflect Jesus to the world, and we have no idea how it might be a seed planted in their lives so they will long know this Jesus as well.

Let us be careful sweet friends to love each other well, to love as Jesus does, and to lead our lives intentionally in such a way that brings glory to him alone. The peace that this kind of love brings is just what the world is seeking today in all the wrong places! With Jesus as our guide, we can love like Him.

Thank you, Lord, for the example Jesus left for us of loving well.
Help me to live this out in my own life even today.

Design Tip

Set a budget! If you enjoy DIY or thrifty type projects, you can save a lot of money doing the work yourself. If not, it's ok to buy a few key pieces and then gradually add more as you save!

Live in Peace

If it is possible, as far as it depends on you, live at peace with everyone.
ROMANS 12:18 ESV

Pursuing peace in our homes is often easier said than done. It's a challenge because peace can be an elusive character anyway.

We live in a world that is anything but peaceful. We may have come from homes that were less than peaceful and the example of marriage may have been lacking. We may have issues with rest and trust. Romans teaches us that as much as we can control, we are to live in peace with each other.

Sometimes it's not possible, and I get that. There can be circumstances beyond our control that make it challenging to live peaceably with each other. And while we can't control our feelings all the time, we can control our reactions. We can make it a practice to not say the first thing that comes to mind when we are emotional. We can make it a practice to step away for a moment when we are angry, and before we unleash a tirade of frustration. We can make it a practice to speak with calmness in our tone and a prayerful undertone beneath our words.

Whatever is within our power—letting go of wrongs, letting go of resentments, watching our reactions, controlling our temper—these are the things that matter and will make a difference in our homes.

Lord, help me to always live peaceably when it is within my power by laying down my rights and letting go of my resentments.

Marriage Tip

Be supportive of one another.

NAOMI MCINTOSH

Make Peace

Let us therefore make every effort to do what leads to peace and to mutual edification.
ROMANS 14:19 NIV

This verse concludes a longer passage regarding the way we are to conduct ourselves with our brothers and sisters in Christ. The rights and freedoms we have been given through the liberty of the grace of Christ do not give us license to cause someone else to stumble. Loving well implies a certain amount of surrender and dying daily.

And this is especially true in our marriages. We love well when we die daily to our selfish nature and desires. Verse 19 concludes this passage of Romans 14 by encouraging us to follow after the things which make for peace and the things that edify. The word edify indicates instruction or encouragement to improve morally or intellectually.

Our marriages are places of refinement. Becoming more like Christ, we work to live in peace and in bettering each other by using our giftedness to its full potential. Whether that giftedness is by acts of mercy or helpfulness, balancing finances, or working a job or career that benefits our home, it's surrendering our will to God's because He placed us in this union. Following His plan brings us peace and we all desire to have that!

Dear Father, thank you for the promise of peace in our acts of loving well. Help me to continue to die to myself and live unto you by following the principles found in your Word.

Find a hobby or activities you like to do together. Having fun and dating your spouse never gets old!

JENNIFER INGRAM

Buried Treasure

For where your treasure is, there will your heart be also.
Matthew 6:21 KJV

As you think, you act. As you build your mind around what is important, you can believe your heart will follow. If you build your heart around hitting certain financial goals, you will always be pursuing a moving target.

Financial concerns can be a major stress factor putting pressure on a marriage. Because opposites attract, usually you'll have a spender and a saver. This is its own challenge but thank goodness for it. If you're both spenders, without some boundaries, you'll be in the poorhouse, and if you are both savers, you might make each other miserable because you never allow for some fun.

Be careful with this pitfall—it's easy for these little molehills to become mountains. Finances and arguments related to finances are one of the top reasons couples cite as the beginning of the end for their relationships. There's a reason the Bible teaches that the love of money is the root of all evil. Money itself is not the problem. The endless pursuit of money causes our hearts to be wrapped up in making money at all costs.

But this buried treasure always comes back to the heart. When our heart is in the right place, the rest of our lives will align too. When we are united in our purpose to love God and love others, the rest of the things will fall into place. Let's be careful in our marriages to keep money its rightful place.

Lord, thank you for the abilities you give us and the opportunity to work.
May we always keep our hearts in pursuit of you first of all so that we will
not have an unhealthy desire for money in our lives.

Maturity

But the fruit of the Spirit is love, joy, peace, patience, kindness, goodness, faithfulness, gentleness, self-control; against such things there is no law.

GALATIANS 5:22–23 ESV

I hate to say it, but one major reason most marriages struggle comes down to lack of maturity and boundaries. Being willing to take responsibility to work on the areas we lack, whether it's a lazy spirit or procrastination, is key to putting your relationship first and building a marriage with a strong foundation. And if you have no boundaries around a past life or love, around the involvement of your parents or in-laws, or even your work, you will face a lot of conflict and struggle in your marriage.

We are told to leave and cleave for a reason, and if you run home to complain about your spouse every time you have a fight, your parents will only believe your spouse to be the worst of himself. Trust me—not the best plan.

If you have no boundaries around your work life and can't keep a promise to come home for dinner or make it to a planned event, you will face incredible stress and pressure. This is not meant to indicate that the occasional long work night or missed event is wrong but watch the pattern. Are you regularly unreliable when it comes to making plans or being home?

We can apply boundaries around our behaviors as well. Whether we struggle with anger, laziness or an ungrateful spirit, bringing these behaviors to the Lord in confession can help us to recognize when we are off course. Being careful to cultivate the fruit of the spirit in our lives personally means that the good crops of love, joy and peace will overflow into our homes!

Oh, Lord, I thank you for the evidence of the Spirit's work in our lives by the harvest of the fruit of love, joy, and peace. What a gift that is!

Marriage Tip

Be quick to forgive. Don't let yourself hold on to grudges or hurt feelings.

United in Love

My goal is that they may be encouraged in heart and united in love, so that they may have the full riches of complete understanding, in order that they may know the mystery of God, namely, Christ, in whom are hidden all the treasures of wisdom and knowledge.

COLOSSIANS 2:2–3 ESV

Isn't "united in love" a beautiful phrase? Our marriages should be marked by not only love but also by unity. Love should be the glue that unites us, rooted and grounded in the love that Christ has for us. There is such depth of wisdom in the vastness of Christ's love. Understanding His love for us and in turn our love for each other is such a beautiful thing.

I'm reminded that no matter what we face in this life, having a partner to face it together is a gift. Whether job loss, financial difficulty, or the daily grind of life, having our spouse on the same page doesn't necessarily make the problems go away, but it sure does make the challenges easier to bear.

In addition, being united in love, we can have a part in advancing the Kingdom. If we are purposed to live this life with intention, we will be doing all we can to leverage our lives for the Kingdom in our marriages. Being united in our love for each other will look so different to the world around us. And they will want to know what makes us different.

Lord, help us to be united in love! Thank you for the gift of marriage and the opportunity to face this life together no matter what comes our way.

Thank You

Thank you to my Contributors for their Design and Marriage Tips and Photography.

Lindsey Bonnice
www.livesweetblog.com
Instagram: @livesweet

Vanessa Hunt
www.atthepicketfence.com
Instagram: @atthepicketfence

Jennifer Ingram
www.gracious-spaces.net
Instagram: @graciousspaces

Julie Lancia and Jodie Kammerer
www.thedesigntwins.com
Instagram: @julie.thedesigntwins
and @jodie.thedesigntwins

Naomi McIntosh
Instagram: @naomimcintoshphotography

Kelly Radcliff
www.thetatteredpew.com
Instagram: @thetatteredpew

Paige Rien
www.paigerien.com
Instagram: @paigerien

Jenny Zacharewicz
Instagram: @bigfamilylittlefarmhouse

About the Author

A multi-passionate creative fueled mostly by coffee, Victoria Duerstock relentlessly pursues her dreams. Writing, speaking, and helping creatives grow their platforms with DIY and done for you solutions keep her busy!

Victoria's mission is to create beauty, cultivate community and leverage all the resources to impact others and leave a legacy.

Other Books by the Author

Heart & Home: Design Basics for Your Living Space

Heart & Home for Christmas: Celebrating Joy in Your Living Space

Extraordinary Hospitality for Ordinary Christians: A Radical Approach to Preparing Your Heart & Home for Gospel Centered Community

Advent Devotions & Christmas Crafts for Families

New in 2021

Revived & Renovated: Real Life Conversations on the Intersection of Home, Faith, and Everything in Between.

Navigating Minefields: A Young Man's Blueprint for Success on Life's Battlefield